Standard Grade | Foundation | General | Credit

Drama

**Foundation/General/Credit
Level 2005**
F/G/C 2005 Stimulus Paper
2005 Exam

**Foundation/General/Credit
Level 2006**
F/G/C 2006 Stimulus Paper
2006 Foundation Exam
2006 General Exam
2006 Credit Exam

**Foundation/General/Credit
Level 2007**
F/G/C 2007 Stimulus Paper
2007 Foundation Exam
2007 General Exam
2007 Credit Exam

**Foundation/General/Credit
Level 2008**
F/G/C 2008 Stimulus Paper
2008 Foundation Exam
2008 General Exam
2008 Credit Exam

Leckie×Leckie

© Scottish Qualifications Authority
All rights reserved. Copying prohibited. No part of this publication may be reproduced, stored in a retrieval system, or
transmitted in any form or by any means, electronic, mechanical, photocopying, recording or otherwise.

First exam published in 2005.
Published by Leckie & Leckie Ltd, 3rd Floor, 4 Queen Street, Edinburgh EH2 1JE
tel: 0131 220 6831 fax: 0131 225 9987 enquiries@leckieandleckie.co.uk www.leckieandleckie.co.uk

ISBN 978-1-84372-627-2

A CIP Catalogue record for this book is available from the British Library.

Leckie & Leckie is a division of Huveaux plc.

Leckie & Leckie is grateful to the copyright holders, as credited at the back of the book, for permission to use their material.
Every effort has been made to trace the copyright holders and to obtain their permission for the use of copyright material.
Leckie & Leckie will gladly receive information enabling them to rectify any error or omission in subsequent editions.

[BLANK PAGE]

F
G
C

0700/402

NATIONAL
QUALIFICATIONS
2005

FRIDAY, 20 MAY
1.00 PM – 2.30 PM

DRAMA
STANDARD GRADE
Foundation, General
and Credit Levels
Stimulus Paper

Study carefully the five stimuli (i), (ii), (iii), (iv) and (v)
before answering questions 1 to 8 in Section A of the
Question Paper.

SCOTTISH
QUALIFICATIONS
AUTHORITY

SAB 0700/402 6/9370

©

STIMULUS (i)

> # "The Best Days of your Life!"

STIMULUS (ii)

Crossroads ahead

STIMULUS (iii)

One for anger, two for mirth,
Three for a wedding and four for a birth
Five for silver, six for gold,
Seven for a secret that shall never be told.

anon

STIMULUS (iv)

The Scream by Edvard Munch (1863–1944), National Gallery, Oslo

[Turn over for Stimulus (v) on *Page four*

STIMULUS (v)

Danforth: Is that document a lie? If it is a lie I will not accept it! What say you? I will not deal in lies, Mister! You will give me your honest confession in my hand, or I cannot keep you from the rope. Which way do you go, Mister? Marshall!

Parris: Proctor, Proctor!

Hale: Man, you will hang! You cannot!

Proctor: I can. And there's your first marvel, that I can. You have made your magic now, for now I do think I see some shred of goodness in John Proctor. Not enough to weave a banner with, but white enough to keep it from such dogs. Give them no tear! Tears pleasure them! Show honour now, show stony heart and sink them with it!

The Crucible by Arthur Miller Act IV

[END OF STIMULUS PAPER]

FOR OFFICIAL USE

F
G
C

Total

0700/401

NATIONAL
QUALIFICATIONS
2005

FRIDAY, 20 MAY
1.00 PM – 2.30 PM

DRAMA
STANDARD GRADE
Foundation, General
and Credit Levels

Fill in these boxes and read what is printed below.

Full name of centre

Town

Forename(s)

Surname

Date of birth
Day Month Year

Scottish candidate number

Number of seat

1 Read each question carefully.

2 Attempt **all** questions in **both** sections.

3 You may use sketches and diagrams to illustrate your answers.

4 All answers are to be written in this answer book. If there is not enough space for you to complete your answer to any question, **additional paper** can be obtained from the invigilator.

5 The Stimuli for Section A are supplied in a separate paper. Check that you have this paper before the examination begins.

6 Before leaving the examination room you must give this book to the invigilator. If you do not, you may lose all the marks for this paper.

SCOTTISH
QUALIFICATIONS
AUTHORITY

©

Marks

SECTION A

Answer **all** of the following questions.

Your answers should be based
on work from the **stimulus material**.
(*A copy of the Stimulus Paper is provided*.)

My group chose stimulus _____ (*enter number from stimulus paper*).

1. Why did your group choose this stimulus?

   _____

   _____   1

   Give **two** ideas offered by your group in response to your chosen stimulus.

   _____

   _____

   _____   2

2. When you were creating your drama, in what **three** ways did you help your group?

   _____

   _____

   _____

   _____

   _____

   _____   3

Marks

3. Write a brief outline of how **your group's** drama starts, develops and finishes. Include the time and place of each scene.

_____

_____

_____

_____

_____

_____

_____

_____

_____

_____

_____

_____

_____

_____

_____

_____

_____

_____

_____

_____

6

4. (a) After you had chosen your stimulus, which part of the process did you spend most time on?

_____

1

(b) Explain why this was and say how you dealt with difficulties.

_____

_____

_____

_____

_____

_____

3

5. (a) Give the name and age of the character played by you.

_____

1

(b) Describe the costume **and** personal props you would have liked to use for your character.

_____

_____

_____

_____

_____

_____

_____

4

(c) What was your character's most important moment in the drama? Why?

_____

_____

_____

_____

2

Marks

5. (continued)

(*d*) At this moment, or leading up to this moment, how did your character speak and move?

_____

_____

_____

_____

_____

_____   **4**

6. Who would make a suitable target audience for your drama? Give **two** reasons for your answer.

_____

_____

_____

_____

_____   **3**

7. Choose **one scene** from your drama. Describe the **mood** and **atmosphere** you would try to create for your audience. Give reasons for your answer.

Scene number _____

_____

_____

_____

_____

_____   **4**

DO NOT
WRITE I
THIS MAR(

Marks

8. Look at the lighting effects below. Imagine that your teacher has asked you to use **four** of them in your drama.

Choose **four** and complete the following.

fade to blackout   **cold colour gel(s)**   **spotlight**   **strobe**

warm colour gel(s)   **snap to blackout**   **cross fade**   **follow spot**

(i)   I would use _____ when _____

_____

because _____

_____

_____ .   4

(ii)   I would use _____ when _____

_____

because _____

_____

_____ .   4

(iii) I would use _____ when _____

_____

because _____

_____

_____ .   4

(iv)   I would use _____ when _____

_____

because _____

_____

_____ .   4

SECTION B

Answer **all** of the following questions.

Your answers should **not** be based
on work from the **stimulus material**.

---

9. Replace the words in brackets with the correct word from the list below.

characters	**flashback**	**rehearsed**	**presentation**
evaluated	**stimulus**	**costume**	**devise**
scenes	**venue**		

On Monday, our teacher gave us a **(starting point for a drama)** ——————

and asked us to **(make up)** ————————————— a drama.

In our group we had lots of ideas but we soon decided on one. We thought of what

(parts) ————————————— we needed and how many **(sections)**

————————————— we should have in the drama.

After we had **(practised a drama)** ————————————— for a

while, we were ready to perform. Our final **(drama prepared for an audience)**

————————————— was shown to the rest of the class. When they

(reviewed) ————————————— it they thought it was really good.

7

[Turn over

DO NOT
WRITE IN
THIS MARG

Marks

10. The diagrams below are of four different **types of staging**.

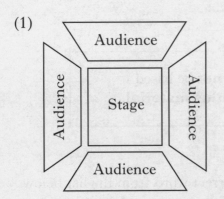

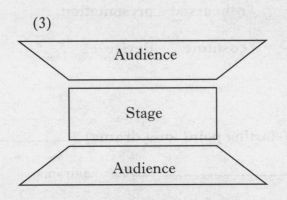

(a) Name each type of staging.

(1) _____

(2) _____

(3) _____

(4) _____

4

(b) Choose **one** type of staging from the four diagrams above. Give an **advantage** of using it.

Diagram number _____

Advantage _____

_____

1

(c) Choose **another** type of staging from the four diagrams above. Give a **disadvantage** of using it.

Diagram number _____

Disadvantage _____

_____

1

Marks

11. Imagine you have been asked to create a piece of drama based on the theme **Trust**.

Use the web below to note down your ideas about this theme. **Two** possible ideas are given.

The web diagram below is to help you with ideas and will not be marked.

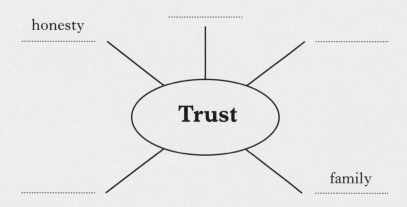

honesty

Trust

family

(*a*) From your ideas above, devise a drama, suitable for acting out, that has **3 scenes**.

Scene 1 (beginning)   Time_____   Place_____

_____

_____

_____

_____

_____

_____

Scene 2 (middle)   Time_____   Place_____

_____

_____

_____

_____

_____

DO NOT
WRITE I
THIS MAR

Mark

11. **(a) (continued)**

Scene 3 (end)   Time _____   Place _____

_____

_____

_____

_____

_____

12

(b) What would your audience find out from **Scene 1** of your drama entitled **Trust**?

_____

_____

_____

_____

_____

_____

4

(c) Give the name, age and occupation of the main character in your drama entitled **Trust**.

_____

_____

_____

2

11. (continued)

(*d*) What is the **role** and **status** of the main character in your drama entitled **Trust**?

_____

_____

_____

_____

4

(*e*) What is the purpose of **one other** character in your drama entitled **Trust**?

_____

_____

2

(*f*) Choose a character from the final scene of your drama. What advice on the use of voice and movement would you give the actor playing this part?

_____

_____

_____

_____

_____

_____

_____

_____

5

[Turn over for Question 11(*g*) on *Page twelve*

11. **(continued)**

(g) In what ways would you use theatre arts to enhance your drama? **What** theatre arts would you use, **when** would you use them and **why**?

_____

_____

_____

_____

_____

_____

_____

_____

_____

_____

_____

_____

_____

_____

_____

_____

_____

_____

8

[END OF QUESTION PAPER]

[BLANK PAGE]

F G C

0700/404

NATIONAL
QUALIFICATIONS
2006

FRIDAY, 19 MAY
F: 9.00 AM – 9.45 AM
G: 10.05 AM – 10.50 AM
C: 11.10 AM – 12.10 PM

DRAMA
STANDARD GRADE
Foundation, General
and Credit Levels
Stimulus Paper

Study carefully the five stimuli (i), (ii), (iii), (iv) and (v) before answering the questions in Section A of the Question Paper.

SCOTTISH
QUALIFICATIONS
AUTHORITY

©

STIMULUS (i)

Truth and Consequences

STIMULUS (ii)

STIMULUS (iii)

As cold as ice
As sharp as a knife
As dead as a doornail

STIMULUS (iv)

Call for Help

The following items were found by a jogger in Homestead Park on Tuesday evening: a mobile phone, a gold watch and an old black and white photograph of a young child. Anyone who thinks they may be able to assist police with their enquiries is requested to contact their local police station.

[Turn over for Stimulus (v) on *Page four*

STIMULUS (v)

TANYA: . . . I went downstairs and outside with the rubbish. It was going to be a lovely day. Blossom on the trees. Spring flowers in the garden. I thought I might pick some and leave them on the table for Stefan to see when he came in. The sun was up in the air. It's hard to explain. At first I thought there had been a frost in the night but it was too warm for frost. There was a little garden outside the block of flats and they had planted roses. The new glossy leaves had this fine white powder on them. Like ash. I touched it. Something else. No birds were singing. None at all . . .

Extract from *Wormwood* by Catherine Czerkawska

[END OF STIMULUS PAPER]

FOR OFFICIAL USE

F

Total

0700/401

NATIONAL
QUALIFICATIONS
2006

FRIDAY, 19 MAY
9.00 AM – 9.45 AM

DRAMA
STANDARD GRADE
Foundation Level

Fill in these boxes and read what is printed below.

Full name of centre

Town

Forename(s)

Surname

Date of birth

Day Month Year   Scottish candidate number   Number of seat

1 Read each question carefully.

2 Attempt **all** questions in **both** sections.

3 You may use sketches and diagrams to illustrate your answers.

4 All answers are to be written in this answer book. If there is not enough space for you to complete your answer to any question, **additional paper** can be obtained from the invigilator.

5 The Stimuli for Section A are supplied in a separate paper. Check that you have this paper before the examination begins.

6 Before leaving the examination room you must give this book to the invigilator. If you do not, you may lose all the marks for this paper.

SCOTTISH
QUALIFICATIONS
AUTHORITY

SA 0700/401 6/4670

Mark.

SECTION A

Answer **all** of the following questions.

Your answers should be based
on work from the **stimulus material**.
(*A copy of the Stimulus Paper is provided.*)

My group chose stimulus _____ (*enter number from Stimulus Paper*).

1. Use the space below to write a **brief scenario** of the drama created by your group.

A **brief** summary of the action	
Beginning	
Middle	
End	

6

Marks

2. Complete the following Character Card for **your character.**

Full name and age: _____   1

Occupation: _____   1

Personality: _____

_____

_____

_____   2

Appearance (eg height, build, style of dress): _____

_____

_____

_____   2

Other information about your character: _____

_____

_____

_____   1

[Turn over

Marks

3. (*a*) What was the **most important moment** in your drama for **your character**?

_____

_____

_____

1

(*b*) Why was this moment important?

_____

_____

_____

1

(*c*) Describe how your character **spoke** at that moment.

_____

_____

_____

_____

2

(*d*) Describe how your character **moved** at that moment.

_____

_____

_____

_____

2

(*e*) Theatre Arts are:

Lighting	**Sound**	**Props**	**Set**	**Costume**	**Make-up**

In what ways would you use **one** of these at this important moment in your drama?

_____

_____

1

Marks

4. In the space below draw a ground plan of the acting area for **one** scene of your drama.

This scene takes place in _____

Key:

5

DO NOT
WRITE **I**
THIS MAR

Mark

SECTION B

Answer **all** of the following questions.

> Your answers should **not** be based
> on work from the **stimulus material**.

5. Read the following questions and put a tick (✓) in the box next to the correct answer.

(*a*) A drama presented through dance moves is a

    mime ☐

    dance drama ☐

    monologue ☐

    convention ☐

(*b*) The speed of movement or speech is called

    body language ☐

    volume ☐

    height ☐

    pace ☐

(*c*) The final rehearsal of a play with all theatre arts is a

    dress rehearsal ☐

    presentation ☐

    technical rehearsal ☐

    practice ☐

(*d*) The outline of the plot of a drama is called a

    script ☐

    scenario ☐

    story ☐

    convention ☐

(*e*) The build up of excitement in a drama is called

    timing ☐

    acting ☐

    tension ☐

    plot ☐

(*f*) The signal for an actor to say or do something is

    dramatic moment ☐

    mime ☐

    sign ☐

    cue ☐

(*g*) When a character shakes a fist they use a

    role-play ☐

    point ☐

    signal ☐

    gesture ☐

7

Marks

6. Look carefully at the two characters in the picture below.

Then answer questions (*a*) to (*h*) which follow.

Read all the questions before starting to write.

Character A   Character B

They are two characters in a drama.

(*a*) Who is character A?

_____   1

(*b*) Who is character B?

_____   1

(*c*) What do you see **happening** in this picture?

_____

_____

_____   2

(*d*) **When** and **where** is this happening?

_____

_____   1

(*e*) What do you think happened **before** this?

_____

_____

_____   2

[Turn over for Questions 6 (continued) and 7 on *Page eight*

DO NOT
WRITE I
THIS MAR

Mark

6. **(continued)**

(f) How do you think character A is feeling?

_____   1

(g) How do you think character B is feeling?

_____   1

(h) What do you think happens next?

_____

_____

_____

_____

_____

_____

_____

_____   3

7. Look at the words below and write them in the correct column.

**musical   flashback   slow motion
pantomime   play   freeze frame**

Drama Form	Drama Convention

6

[END OF QUESTION PAPER]

FOR OFFICIAL USE

G

Total

0700/402

NATIONAL
QUALIFICATIONS
2006

FRIDAY, 19 MAY
10.05 AM – 10.50 AM

DRAMA
STANDARD GRADE
General Level

Fill in these boxes and read what is printed below.

Full name of centre

Town

Forename(s)

Surname

Date of birth
Day Month Year

Scottish candidate number

Number of seat

Read each question carefully.

Attempt **all** questions.

Write your answers in the space provided on the question paper.

Write as neatly as possible.

Answer in sentences wherever possible.

Before leaving the examination room you must give this book to the invigilator. If you do not, you may lose all the marks for this paper.

SCOTTISH
QUALIFICATIONS
AUTHORITY

DO NOT
WRITE I
THIS MAR

Mark.

SECTION A

Answer **all** of the following questions.

> Your answers should be based
> on work from the **stimulus material**.
> (*A copy of the Stimulus Paper is provided.*)

My group chose stimulus _____ (*enter number from stimulus paper*).

1. Use the space below to write a **brief scenario** of the drama created by your group.

Scene number	Time, place and action

6

Marks

2. (*a*) List **three** characters in the drama including your own.

Give the role of each.

Your character _____

Role _____

Character 2 _____

Role _____

Character 3 _____

Role _____

3

(*b*) Look at the list above. Describe the relationship between **your character** and character 2 **or** character 3.

_____

_____

_____

_____

2

(*c*) Describe in what ways voice and movement were used to show this relationship.

_____

_____

_____

_____

3

[Turn over

| | *Marks* |

3. Complete the following for a character played by **another member of your group**.

Full Name: _____ Age: _____   **1**

Occupation: _____   **1**

Physical Description: _____

_____

_____

_____   **2**

Personality: _____

_____

_____

_____   **2**

Costume: _____

_____

_____

_____   **3**

Personal props: _____

_____

_____

_____   **3**

Marks

4.

> **You have developed your drama from stimulus ⟶ final evaluation.**

What challenges did you and your group face during this process and how did you deal with them?

_____

_____

_____

_____

_____

_____

_____

_____

4

[Turn over

DO NOT
WRITE IN
THIS MARG

Marks

SECTION B

Answer **all** of the following questions.

> Your answers should **not** be based on work from the
> **stimulus material**.

5. Read the following scenario.

    Scene 1 In a supermarket 11.30 pm.
    Danny is being led away by the police.
    His friends are cheering and Danny could not care less.

    Scene 2 Outside court building 10.30 am the next day.
    Danny walks down the steps to be met by his mother.
    His friends are not there.

    Describe Danny's **voice and movement** in each scene.

    Scene 1 _____

    _____

    _____

    _____

    _____

    _____

    _____   5

    Scene 2 _____

    _____

    _____

    _____

    _____

    _____

    _____   5

Marks

6. Explain what is meant by the drama term *Mime*.

Mime is _____   2

Now complete the words below.

To be effectively performed, *mime* should be:

S _____   1

P _____   1

E _____   1

C _____   1

S _____   1

7. Complete the grid below by adding in the correct **areas of the stage**.

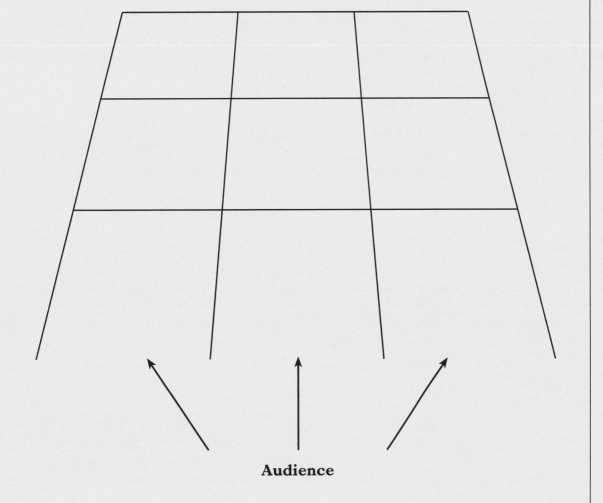

Audience   3

Marks

8.

Emily Carruthers, 72, sits alone in her favourite chair. She is leafing through her photograph album.

This is the start of a drama. Describe the set/set dressings, lighting and sound to accompany this opening stage picture.

Set/set dressings _____

_____

_____

_____

_____

_____

_____

_____

4

Lighting _____

_____

_____

_____

_____

3

Marks

8. **(continued)**

Sound _____

_____

_____

_____

_____

_____

3

[*END OF QUESTION PAPER*]

[BLANK PAGE]

C

FOR OFFICIAL USE

Total ☐

0700/403

NATIONAL
QUALIFICATIONS
2006

FRIDAY, 19 MAY
11.10 AM – 12.10 PM

DRAMA
STANDARD GRADE
Credit Level

Fill in these boxes and read what is printed below.

Full name of centre

Town

Forename(s)

Surname

Date of birth
Day Month Year   Scottish candidate number   Number of seat

1 Read each question carefully.

2 Attempt **all** questions in **both** sections.

3 You may use sketches and diagrams to illustrate your answers.

4 All answers are to be written in this answer book. If there is not enough space for you to complete your answer to any question, **additional paper** can be obtained from the invigilator.

5 The Stimuli for Section A are supplied in a separate paper. Check that you have this paper before the examination begins.

6 Before leaving the examination room you must give this book to the invigilator. If you do not, you may lose all the marks for this paper.

SCOTTISH
QUALIFICATIONS
AUTHORITY

SA 0700/403 6/6370   ©

SECTION A

Marks

Answer **all** of the following questions.

> Your answers should be based
> on work from the **stimulus material**.
> (*A copy of the Stimulus Paper is provided.*)

My group chose stimulus _____ (*enter number from Stimulus Paper*).

> *"The purpose of a drama must be established
> in order to communicate a meaning."*

1. (*a*) What was the purpose of your drama?

_____   1

(*b*) Did your drama achieve this purpose? How did you know?

_____

_____

_____

_____

_____   2

2. (*a*) Which part of the plot do you feel was communicated most effectively?

_____

_____   1

(*b*) Explain why this was the case.

_____

_____

_____

_____

_____

_____   3

3. (*a*) Which **character** was, in your opinion, portrayed most successfully?

_____

1

(*b*) Explain how the **actor** achieved this.

_____

_____

_____

_____

_____

_____

_____

_____

_____

_____

4

[Turn over

DO NO'
WRITE
THIS MAR

Mark

4. How could you have used theatre arts to enhance two key moments in your drama? Use a different theatre art for each moment and justify your answer.

Moment 1 _____

_____

_____

_____

_____

_____

_____

_____

_____

4

Moment 2 _____

_____

_____

_____

_____

_____

_____

_____

_____

_____

4

Marks

SECTION B

Answer **all** of the following questions.

> Your answers should **not** be based
> on work from the **stimulus material**.

5. "*Tension is the driving force of a drama.*"

(*a*) List **five** ways in which tension can be created.

1 _____

2 _____

3 _____

4 _____

5 _____   5

(*b*) Explain how Dramatic Tension was used in a drama in which you took part
during your Standard Grade Drama Course.
You may wish to expand on, or add to, your answer to 5 (*a*).

_____

_____

_____

_____

_____

_____

_____

_____

_____

_____

_____   8

[Turn over

DO NOT
WRITE I
THIS MAR

Mark

6. Write the correct word after each definition.

(*a*) Appropriate speech for the person being spoken to. _____

(*b*) Audience seated on two sides of the acting area. _____

(*c*) To remove all the set from the acting area. _____

(*d*) One actor unintentionally preventing
another from being seen by the audience. _____

(*e*) Lantern giving a hard edged beam of light. _____   **5**

7.

Name **five** items of stage make-up needed to create this character of a tramp.

1 _____

2 _____

3 _____

4 _____

5 _____   **5**

Marks

8. Imagine that your group has been asked to devise a drama entitled

"World in Danger"

(*a*) Write a scenario of a drama, suitable for acting out.
Include time, place and key characters/relationships.

_____

_____

_____

_____

_____

_____

_____

_____

_____

_____

_____

_____

_____

_____

_____

_____

_____

_____

8

Mark

8. (continued)

(b) Think of the overall style or design concepts for your drama.
Describe in what ways **set** and **costume** would add to the overall effect you wish to communicate to your audience.

_____

_____

_____

_____

_____

_____

_____

_____

_____

_____

_____

_____

_____

_____

7

Marks

8. **(continued)**

   (*c*) Describe what you consider to be the climax or key event in your drama.
   Say why.

   _____

   _____

   _____

   _____

   _____

2

   (*d*) Imagine this moment as a **tableau**. Describe how it would look.

   _____

   _____

   _____

   _____

   _____

   _____

   _____

   _____

   _____

   _____

[Turn over

4

Mark

8. (continued)

(e) Choose **two** from the following list. Describe how you might use them and how each would enhance the impact of the tableau.

Use of levels	SFX	Props	Voice-over	LFX

_____

_____

_____

_____

_____

_____

_____

_____

_____

_____

_____

_____

_____

_____

6

[END OF QUESTION PAPER]

[BLANK PAGE]

F G C

0700/404

NATIONAL QUALIFICATIONS 2007	TUESDAY, 15 MAY F: 9.00 AM – 9.45 AM G: 10.05 AM – 10.50 AM C: 11.10 AM – 12.10 PM	DRAMA STANDARD GRADE Foundation, General and Credit Levels Stimulus Paper

Study carefully the five stimuli (i), (ii), (iii), (iv) and (v) before answering the questions in Section A of the Question Paper.

SCOTTISH
QUALIFICATIONS
AUTHORITY

STIMULUS (i)

Confessed faults are half mended.

Scottish Proverb

STIMULUS (ii)

Flight
Quint Buchholz

STIMULUS (iii)

Like curs a glance has brought to heel, . . .
We listen'd flinching there:
And look'd, and look'd, on the untouched meal
And the overtoppled chair.

Wilfred Wilson Gibson (Flannan Isle)

STIMULUS (iv)

1. **neb**: Another word for nose: "Jist you keep yer neb oot o' this."

(Scots Dictionary)

[Turn over for Stimulus (v) on *Page four*

STIMULUS (v)

ONCE IN A LIFETIME OPPORTUNITY!

Generate a substantial income and build yourself a worthwhile pension. Part time/full time involvement in an ethical, reputable and proven marketing campaign in preventative medicine. Moderate outlay (5/20K + VAT)

For details ring Freephone 0800 555 1212

Dreams can come true

FOR SALE

Wedding dress (white) size 14. Never worn.

Companion Wanted

To share car and help pay fuel.
Leaving for London soon.

TELEPHONE PROFITS

* Horoscope * Tarot *

You are paid
for every call received.
No equipment required
No training required

[END OF STIMULUS PAPER]

FOR OFFICIAL USE

F

Total

0700/401

NATIONAL
QUALIFICATIONS
2007

TUESDAY, 15 MAY
9.00 AM – 9.45 AM

DRAMA
STANDARD GRADE
Foundation Level

Fill in these boxes and read what is printed below.

Full name of centre

Town

Forename(s)

Surname

Date of birth

Day Month Year

Scottish candidate number

Number of seat

1 Read each question carefully.

2 Attempt **all** questions in **both** sections.

3 You may use sketches and diagrams to illustrate your answers.

4 All answers are to be written in this answer book. If there is not enough space for you to complete your answer to any question, **additional paper** can be obtained from the invigilator.

5 The Stimuli for Section A are supplied in a separate paper. Check that you have this paper before the examination begins.

6 Before leaving the examination room you must give this book to the invigilator. If you do not, you may lose all the marks for this paper.

SCOTTISH
QUALIFICATIONS
AUTHORITY

SA 0700/401 6/6170

©

DO NOT
WRITE II
THIS MARG

Marks

SECTION A

Answer **all** of the following questions.

> Your answers should be based
> on work from the **stimulus material**.
> (*A copy of the Stimulus Paper is provided.*)

My group chose stimulus _____ (*enter number from Stimulus Paper*).

1. Think back to the story of the drama created by your group.

   (*a*) What happened at the beginning of your drama?

   3

   (*b*) What happened at the end of your drama?

   3

2. Complete the following Character Card for **your character.**

Full name and age: _____   1

Occupation: _____   1

Appearance: _____

_____

_____

_____   3

Name **two** items of costume for your character:

_____

_____   2

Name **one** personal prop for your character:

_____   1

[Turn over

DO NOT
WRITE IN
THIS MARG

Marks

3. Read all of the parts of this question before you start to write.

Think back to the drama created by your group.

(*a*) Which part of the action was the most dramatic?

_____

_____ 1

(*b*) Give a reason for your answer.

_____

_____ 1

(*c*) Name a character in that part of the action.

_____ 1

(*d*) How did that character **speak** in that part of the action?

_____

_____

_____ 2

(*e*) How did that character **move** in that part of the action?

_____

_____

_____ 2

Marks

3. (continued)

(*f*) Theatre arts are:

Lighting	Sound	Props	Set	Costume	Make-up

Choose two of these you would like to use at this dramatic part of the action.

This is how I would use them and why:

Theatre art 1

_____

_____

_____

2

Theatre art 2

_____

_____

_____

2

[Turn over

SECTION B

Answer **all** of the following questions.

> Your answers should **not** be based
> on work from the **stimulus material**.

4. Here is a ground plan.

Look at it carefully and answer the questions on the opposite page.

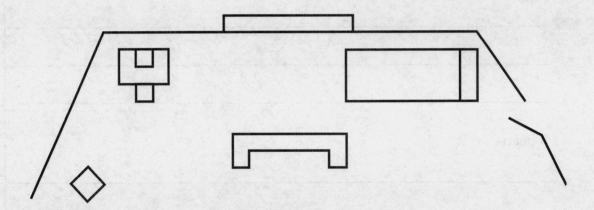

Audience

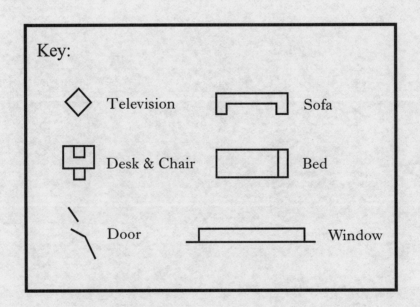

Key:

◇	Television	⊏⊐	Sofa
⊔	Desk & Chair	▭	Bed
╲	Door	▭	Window

4.   (continued)

(a) The door is
(Tick (✓) **one** box.)

☐ USR
☐ DSR
☐ CSL

1

(b) The sofa is
(Tick (✓) **one** box.)

☐ USL
☐ CSR
☐ CS

1

(c) The desk and chair are
(Tick (✓) **one** box.)

☐ USR
☐ DSL
☐ CSR

1

(d) Where is the television? _____

1

(e) Where is the bed? _____

1

(f) Where is the window? _____

1

[Turn over

DO NOT
WRITE I
THIS MAR(

Mark:

5. Imagine this is the opening scene of a drama.

>*A public park.*
>*It is sunny and hot.*

This is a drawing of the set.

Two characters are about to enter.

(*a*) Who might they be?

Character 1 _____

Character 2 _____   **2**

(*b*) Why might they be there?

Character 1 (*reason*) _____

_____

Character 2 (*reason*) _____

_____   **2**

(*c*) In what two ways would you like to **light** this scene, and why?

1 _____

Reason _____

2 _____

Reason _____   **4**

Marks

5.   (continued)

(*d*)   In what two ways would you like to use **sound** in this scene, and why?

1 _____

Reason _____

2 _____

Reason _____   **4**

[Turn over for Question 6 on *Page ten*

6. Write the correct word(s) in the space provided.

   (a) A drama which includes song and/or music is a _____   1

   (b) The people watching a drama are called the_____   1

   (c) Clothes worn by actors for their character are called_____   1

   (d) To leave the acting area is to _____   1

   (e) Blocks or platforms used to create levels are called_____   1

   (f) A stage with the audience seated on three sides of the acting area is called

   _____   1

   (g) Movement performed at a slowed down speed is called_____   1

[END OF QUESTION PAPER]

FOR OFFICIAL USE

G

Total

0700/402

NATIONAL
QUALIFICATIONS
2007

TUESDAY, 15 MAY
10.05 AM – 10.50 AM

DRAMA
STANDARD GRADE
General Level

Fill in these boxes and read what is printed below.

Full name of centre

Town

Forename(s)

Surname

Date of birth

Day Month Year   Scottish candidate number   Number of seat

1 Read each question carefully.

2 Attempt **all** questions in **both** sections.

3 You may use sketches and diagrams to illustrate your answers.

4 All answers are to be written in this answer book. If there is not enough space for you to complete your answer to any question, **additional paper** can be obtained from the invigilator.

5 The Stimuli for Section A are supplied in a separate paper. Check that you have this paper before the examination begins.

6 Before leaving the examination room you must give this book to the invigilator. If you do not, you may lose all the marks for this paper.

SECTION A

Mark:

Answer **all** of the following questions.

```
Your answers should be based
on work from the stimulus material.
(A copy of the Stimulus Paper is provided.)
```

My group chose stimulus _____ (*enter number from stimulus paper*).

1.   Use the space below to write a **brief scenario** of the drama created by your group.

Scene number	Time, place and action

6

Page two

Marks

2. (*a*)   What was your character's **role** in the drama?

_____   1

(*b*)   What was the most important moment in the drama for your character?

_____   1

(*c*)   Why was this the most important moment for your character?

_____   1

3.   Think of another character present at that moment.

Complete the following Character Card for that other character.

Full Name: _____ Age: _____   1

Occupation: _____   1

Physical Description: _____

_____

_____   2

Personality: _____

_____

_____

_____   3

4.   Describe the relationship between your character and any other character in your drama. Give reasons for that relationship.

_____

_____

_____

_____   3

5. Think back to your group's drama.

In what ways would you have liked to use **two** of the following to enhance your drama and why?

lighting	**voice over**	**flashback**	**SFX**
	freeze frame	**music**	

_____

_____

_____

_____

_____

_____

_____

_____

6

Marks

6. Look at the following voice words. Select **five** and say when they were used in your group's drama.

clarity   accent   emphasis   volume   pause   pitch   tone

(*a*) _____ was used when _____

_____

1

(*b*) _____ was used when _____

_____

1

(*c*) _____ was used when _____

_____

1

(*d*) _____ was used when _____

_____

1

(*e*) _____ was used when _____

_____

1

[Turn over

Marks

SECTION B

Answer **all** of the following questions.

> Your answers should **not** be based on work from the
> **stimulus material**.

7. Give the correct drama term for the following definitions.

   Insert your answers in the spaces provided below.

   (i) This person tells part(s) of the drama_____   **1**

   (ii) A lantern giving a hard-edged beam of light_____   **1**

   (iii) Change of voice to express emotion_____   **1**

   (iv) Keeping an even distribution of weight _____   **1**

   (v) Place where a drama is presented_____   **1**

   (vi) The written words of a drama_____   **1**

8. Read the following script then answer the questions below.

A: **You've got to help me!**
B: **Why should I?**
A: **You can't mean that. After all I've done for you.**
B: **Oh, I might have known you'd bring that up.**
A: **Please. I'm desperate.**
B: **Well . . .**

(*a*) Who are the characters?

_____

_____

2

(*b*) **"Oh, I might have known you'd bring that up".** What do you think has happened between these two characters in the past?

_____

_____

_____

_____

_____

_____

3

(*c*) Which of the two characters do you think has the higher status and why?

_____

_____

_____

_____

_____

3

[Turn over

DO NOT
WRITE IN
THIS MARG

Marks

8.   **(continued)**

(d)   In what ways could facial expression, body language and gesture be used to show the status of **both** characters?

Facial expression _____

_____

_____

3

Body language _____

_____

_____

3

Gesture _____

_____

_____

3

9. The diagrams below are of three different types of staging.

(*a*)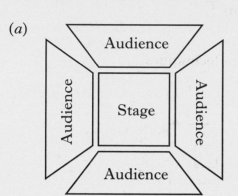

(*b*)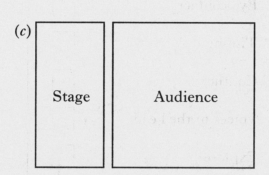

(*c*)

Name each type of staging.

(*a*) _____ **1**

(*b*) _____ **1**

(*c*) _____ **1**

[Turn over for Question 10 on *Page ten*

Marks

10.   **"A variety of techniques can be used in the investigation of characterisation."**

In the list below are four of these characterisation technqiues.

Identify the **four** by ticking the correct boxes.

1.	Posture	☐
2.	Hot-seating	☐
3.	Eye contact	☐
4.	Timing	☐
5.	Conflict	☐
6.	Voices in the head	☐
7.	Explore	☐
8.	Writing in role	☐
9.	Character cards	☐

4

[END OF QUESTION PAPER]

FOR OFFICIAL USE

C

Total

0700/403

NATIONAL
QUALIFICATIONS
2007

TUESDAY, 15 MAY
11.10 AM – 12.10 PM

DRAMA
STANDARD GRADE
Credit Level

Fill in these boxes and read what is printed below.

Full name of centre

Town

Forename(s)

Surname

Date of birth

Day Month Year   Scottish candidate number   Number of seat

1 Read each question carefully.

2 Attempt **all** questions in **both** sections.

3 You may use sketches and diagrams to illustrate your answers.

4 All answers are to be written in this answer book. If there is not enough space for you to complete your answer to any question, **additional paper** can be obtained from the invigilator.

5 The Stimuli for Section A are supplied in a separate paper. Check that you have this paper before the examination begins.

6 Before leaving the examination room you must give this book to the invigilator. If you do not, you may lose all the marks for this paper.

SCOTTISH
QUALIFICATIONS
AUTHORITY

©

Mark

SECTION A

Answer **all** of the following questions.

> Your answers should be based
> on work from the **stimulus material**.
> (*A copy of the Stimulus Paper is provided.*)

My group chose stimulus _____ (*enter number from Stimulus Paper*).

1. (*a*) Identify the central character in your drama.

Name _____ Age _____   1

(*b*) Why was this character central to the drama?

_____

_____

_____

_____   3

(*c*) Now think about the other characters in your drama. Choose any **two** and explain their purpose in the drama.

_____

_____

_____

_____

_____

_____   4

Marks

2. Think about the purpose or message of your drama. How did the plot help to communicate this purpose or message?

_____

_____

_____

_____

_____

_____

_____

6

3. (a) What aspect of your presented drama had the greatest impact on your audience and why?

_____

_____

_____

2

(b) In what ways could theatre arts enhance this impact?

_____

_____

_____

_____

_____

_____

_____

4

[Turn over

DO NO
WRITE
THIS MAR

Mark

SECTION B

Answer **all** of the following questions.

> Your answers should **not** be based
> on work from the **stimulus material**.

4. Give the definitions of the following drama terms.

   (*a*) Barn doors _____

   _____   **2**

   (*b*) Blocking _____

   _____   **2**

   (*c*) Cyclorama _____

   _____   **2**

   (*d*) Intonation _____

   _____   **2**

   (*e*) Wings _____

   _____   **2**

Marks

5. This question requires an imaginative response from you.
   Read carefully all parts of the question, (*a*) to (*e*), before starting to write.

> *A wild Scottish moor.*
> *Thunder and lightning.*
> *Night.*
> *Enter three characters.*

(*a*) Describe the mood and atmosphere you would wish to create at the start of the drama.

_____

(*b*) How could this mood and atmosphere be created through what the audience **sees** before the characters enter?

_____

_____

_____

_____

_____

_____

4

(*c*) How could this mood and atmosphere be created through what the audience **hears** before the characters enter?

_____

_____

_____

_____

_____

_____

4

[Turn over

5. (continued)

Mark

(d) How could this mood and atmosphere be created through the ways in which the three characters make their entrance?

_____

_____

_____

_____

_____

_____

4

(e) Describe how the three characters might look. Your answer must refer to physical description, make-up and costume. You may also include other visual information.

_____

_____

_____

_____

_____

_____

_____

_____

_____

_____

_____

_____

_____

_____

_____

10

6. Identify the following ground plan symbols.

(a) ～～～～～～　　　_____　　1

(b)　　_____　　1

(c)　　_____　　1

(d)　　_____　　1

(e)　　_____　　1

(f)　　_____　　1

[Turn over for Question 7 on *Page eight*

DO NOT
WRITE I
THIS MAR

Mark

7.   **"Conventions are alternative ways of presenting parts of a drama."**

Describe how conventions were effectively used during your Standard Grade course. You must refer to **three** different conventions. (These need not all come from the same drama.)

Convention 1 _____

_____

_____

_____

_____

_____   **4**

Convention 2 _____

_____

_____

_____

_____

_____   **4**

Convention 3 _____

_____

_____

_____

_____

_____   **4**

[END OF QUESTION PAPER]

[BLANK PAGE]

FGC

0700/404

NATIONAL
QUALIFICATIONS
2008

TUESDAY, 20 MAY
F: 9.00 AM – 9.45 AM
G: 10.05 AM – 10.50 AM
C: 11.10 AM – 12.10 PM

DRAMA
STANDARD GRADE
Foundation, General
and Credit Levels
Stimulus Paper

Study carefully the five stimuli (i), (ii), (iii), (iv) and (v) before answering the questions in Section A of the Question Paper.

STIMULUS (i)

"Silver dance shoes in her pocket,
No one's photo in her locket"

The Lady of Shallot by Liz Lochhead

STIMULUS (ii)

STIMULUS (iii)

And so even though we face the difficulties of today and tomorrow, I still have a dream. It is a dream deeply rooted in the American dream.

I have a dream that one day this nation will rise up and live out the true meaning of its creed: "We hold these truths to be self-evident, that all men are created equal."

Martin Luther King Jr., Speech at Civil Rights March on Washington, August 28, 1963

STIMULUS (iv)

Urgent! Phone home asap.

[Turn over for Stimulus (v) on *Page four*

STIMULUS (v)

MAGGIE:	Whit kind o talk is this, Jenny? Did ye no think o us. Yer daddy an me?
JENNY:	Think o ye? Oh aye, Mammy, I thought o ye. But thinking jist made me greet. I was that ashamed o masel . . . Isa and me, we were that rotten tae ye, the things we said.
MAGGIE:	That's a bye, Jenny.
JENNY:	Naethin's ever *bye,* Mammy; it's a there, like a photy-album in yer heid . . . I kept seein ma daddy, the way he used tae sing tae me when I wis wee; I seen him holdin ma bare feet in his hands tae warm them an feedin me bread an hot milk oot o a blue cup. (*Pause*) I don't know where you were, Mammy.
LILY:	Ben the back room wi the midwife, likely. (*Pause*) It's as weel ye came tae yer senses; yon's no the way tae tak oot o yer troubles; a river. But ye're daein fine noo? Ye merriet?
JENNY:	No.

Act III *Men Should Weep* by Ena Lamont Stewart

[END OF STIMULUS PAPER]

FOR OFFICIAL USE

F

Total

0700/401

NATIONAL
QUALIFICATIONS
2008

TUESDAY, 20 MAY
9.00 AM – 9.45 AM

DRAMA
STANDARD GRADE
Foundation Level

Fill in these boxes and read what is printed below.

Full name of centre

Town

Forename(s)

Surname

Date of birth

Day Month Year   Scottish candidate number   Number of seat

1 Read each question carefully.

2 Attempt **all** questions in **both** sections.

3 You may use sketches and diagrams to illustrate your answers.

4 All answers are to be written in this answer book. If there is not enough space for you to complete your answer to any question, **additional paper** can be obtained from the invigilator.

5 The Stimuli for Section A are supplied in a separate paper. Check that you have this paper before the examination begins.

6 Before leaving the examination room you must give this book to the invigilator. If you do not, you may lose all the marks for this paper.

DO NOT
WRITE IN
THIS MARG

SECTION A

Marks

Answer **all** of the following questions.

> Your answers should be based
> on work from the **stimulus material**.
> (*A copy of the Stimulus Paper is provided.*)

My group chose stimulus _____ (*enter number from Stimulus Paper*).

1. How many scenes were in your drama?

_____

1

2. (*a*) Describe what happened in **one** scene that you were in.

_____

_____

_____

_____

_____

3

(*b*) What music **or** sound effect would you like to have used in this scene?
Say why.

_____

_____

_____

2

3. Complete the following information for **your character.**

Full name: _____ Age: _____   **1**

Occupation: _____   **1**

Appearance: _____

_____

_____

_____   **3**

Describe the costume worn by your character.

_____

_____

_____

_____   **3**

[Turn over

DO NOT
WRITE IN
THIS MARG

Marks

4. (a) What was the **most important moment** in your drama for **your character**?

_____

_____   1

    (b) Why was that moment important?

_____

_____   1

    (c) How did your character **speak** and/or **move** at that moment?

_____

_____

_____

_____

_____

_____

_____   4

Marks

5. In the space below draw a ground plan of the acting area for **one** scene of your drama.

This scene takes place in _____

5

Key:

5

 [Turn over

Marks

SECTION B

Answer **all** of the following questions.

Your answers should **not** be based
on work from the **stimulus material**.

6. Look at the words below and write **seven** of them in the appropriate columns.

| Fade in | Exit | Jewellery | Flood | Fade down |
| Thrust | Hats | Gel | Blackout | Scene |

Lighting	Sound	Costume

7

Page six

[Turn over for Question 7 on *Page eight*

Marks

7. Look carefully at the characters pictured below.

   Now read questions (*a*) to (*h*) before writing your answers.

Character A   Character B

(*a*) Who do you think these two characters are?

Character A _____   1

Character B _____   1

Imagine that these two characters are entering a lift in a large office building.

(*b*) Choose either character A **or** B. Describe their movement.

   _____

   _____

   _____   2

Marks

7. **(continued)**

Imagine one character speaks to the other.

(c) What might they say?

_____   1

(d) How might they say it?

_____   1

The lift suddenly stops between floors.

(e) Choose either character A **or** B. Describe their movement.

_____

_____

_____   2

Imagine one character speaks to the other now.

(f) What might they say now?

_____   1

(g) How might they say it?

_____   1

(h) What do you think will happen next to these two characters?

_____

_____

_____   2

[Turn over

DO NOT
WRITE IN
THIS MARG

8. Read the following questions and put a tick (✓) in the box next to the correct answer.

Marks

(a) Loudness or quietness of the voice

- [ ] dialogue
- [ ] monologue
- [ ] volume
- [ ] clarity

(b) A movement of the hand or arm which communicates a meaning or emotion

- [ ] body language
- [ ] gesture
- [ ] cue
- [ ] pace

(c) The speed of speech or movement

- [ ] pace
- [ ] accent
- [ ] intonation
- [ ] practice

(d) A look on a face which shows emotion

- [ ] scenario
- [ ] smile
- [ ] eye contact
- [ ] facial expression

(e) Way of speaking used in a local area or country

- [ ] tone
- [ ] accent
- [ ] tension
- [ ] fluency

(f) Messages given by the position or movement of body

- [ ] convention
- [ ] mime
- [ ] body language
- [ ] gesture

6

[END OF QUESTION PAPER]

FOR OFFICIAL USE

G

Total

0700/402

NATIONAL
QUALIFICATIONS
2008

TUESDAY, 20 MAY
10.05 AM – 10.50 AM

DRAMA
STANDARD GRADE
General Level

Fill in these boxes and read what is printed below.

Full name of centre

Town

Forename(s)

Surname

Date of birth

Day Month Year

Scottish candidate number

Number of seat

1 Read each question carefully.

2 Attempt **all** questions in **both** sections.

3 You may use sketches and diagrams to illustrate your answers.

4 All answers are to be written in this answer book. If there is not enough space for you to complete your answer to any question, **additional paper** can be obtained from the invigilator.

5 The Stimuli for Section A are supplied in a separate paper. Check that you have this paper before the examination begins.

6 Before leaving the examination room you must give this book to the invigilator. If you do not, you may lose all the marks for this paper.

[BLANK PAGE]

Marks

SECTION A

Answer **all** of the following questions.

> Your answers should be based
> on work from the **stimulus material**.
> (*A copy of the Stimulus Paper is provided.*)

My group chose stimulus _____ (*enter number from stimulus paper*).

1. Use the space below to write a **brief scenario** of the drama created by your group.

Scene number	Time, place and action

6

[Turn over

DO NOT
WRITE
THIS MAR

Mark

2. Think about the most important relationship between **your character** and **one other character**.

(*a*) What was the relationship between these two characters?

_____

_____

_____   2

(*b*) Complete the following character information for **that other** character.

Name of character:_____ Age:_____   1

Occupation: _____   1

Physical Description: _____

_____

_____   2

Personality: _____

_____

_____   2

(*c*) What was the **most important moment** in your drama for the relationship between these two characters? Why?

_____

_____

_____

_____

_____   3

Marks

2. **(continued)**

(*d*) How did you and the other actor use voice and movement to highlight the importance of **that moment**?

_____

_____

_____

_____

_____

_____

_____

_____

_____

_____

6

[Turn over

Mark.

3. Look at the following **theatre arts** terms. Select **four** of these and say when you could have used them in your group's drama.

follow spot	live (SFX)	cross fade
rostra	stage make up	personal prop

(a) _____ could have been used when _____

_____

1

(b) _____ could have been used when_____

_____

1

(c) _____ could have been used when_____

_____

1

(d) _____ could have been used when_____

_____

1

4. What would have been the ideal venue and target audience for your drama? Say why.

_____

_____

_____

_____

_____

3

Marks

SECTION B

Answer **all** of the following questions.

> Your answers should **not** be based on work from the
> **stimulus material**.

5.   Complete the following definitions.

(*a*)   Stage within an enclosing arch.

_____   1

(*b*)   Change of voice to express emotion.

_____   1

(*c*)   Recall of words said about a character or situation.

_____   1

(*d*)   A conversation between two or more characters.

_____   1

(*e*)   Questioning a character in role.

_____   1

(*f*)   Drama created 'on the spot' without a script or plan.

_____   1

[Turn over

DO NOT
WRITE IN
THIS MARG

Marks

6. *A ground plan is a bird's eye view of the set.*

A fully correct ground plan must include certain details. List **five** of these.

(i) _____   1

(ii) _____   1

(iii) _____   1

(iv) _____   1

(v) _____   1

7. *The purpose of a drama must be established in order to communicate meaning.*

List **three** examples of purpose.

(i) _____   1

(ii) _____   1

(iii) _____   1

Marks

Read the following question carefully before answering parts (*a*) and (*b*).

8.   Imagine that you have been asked to devise a **movement piece** in two scenes under the following titles.

   Scene 1   Lost in the City

   Scene 2   Found

   (*a*)   Describe in detail the **movement** in each of these two scenes.

   Scene 1 _____

   _____

   _____

   _____

   _____

   _____

   _____

   _____   4

   Scene 2 _____

   _____

   _____

   _____

   _____

   _____

   _____

   _____   4

[Turn over

8.   (continued)

(*b*)   How would you use **theatre arts** to enhance this movement piece?   Indicate
which theatre arts you would use, when you would use them and why.   Refer to
at least two theatre arts in your answer.

_____

_____

_____

_____

_____

_____

_____

_____

_____

_____

_____

_____

_____

8

[END OF QUESTION PAPER]

FOR OFFICIAL USE

C

Total

0700/403

NATIONAL
QUALIFICATIONS
2008

TUESDAY, 20 MAY
11.10 AM – 12.10 PM

**DRAMA
STANDARD GRADE**
Credit Level

Fill in these boxes and read what is printed below.

Full name of centre

Town

Forename(s)

Surname

Date of birth

Day Month Year Scottish candidate number Number of seat

1 Read each question carefully.

2 Attempt **all** questions in **both** sections.

3 You may use sketches and diagrams to illustrate your answers.

4 All answers are to be written in this answer book. If there is not enough space for you to complete your answer to any question, **additional paper** can be obtained from the invigilator.

5 The Stimuli for Section A are supplied in a separate paper. Check that you have this paper before the examination begins.

6 Before leaving the examination room you must give this book to the invigilator. If you do not, you may lose all the marks for this paper.

DO NOT
WRITE IN
THIS MARG

Marks

SECTION A

Answer **all** of the following questions.

> Your answers should be based
> on work from the **stimulus material**.
> (*A copy of the Stimulus Paper is provided*.)

My group chose stimulus _____ (*enter number from Stimulus Paper*).

1. (a) Identify the main strength of your final presentation.

    _____   1

    (b) Which aspect of the drama process contributed most to this?

    _____

    _____   1

    (c) Give reasons for your answer.

    _____

    _____

    _____   2

2. (a) Identify the main weakness of your final presentation.

    _____   1

    (b) Which aspect of the drama process contributed most to this?

    _____

    _____   1

    (c) Give reasons for your answer.

    _____

    _____

    _____   2

Marks

3. *(a)* Name **two** characters of differing status in your drama.

Character 1 _____

Character 2 _____

(b) Describe the status of each character.

Character 1 _____

_____

_____

_____

2

Character 2 _____

_____

_____

_____

2

(c) How was this difference in status shown in performance?

_____

_____

_____

_____

_____

_____

_____

_____

4

(d) Write 'in role' how the character **played by you** felt about one of those characters.

_____

_____

_____

_____

_____

_____

_____

_____

4

Marks

SECTION B

Answer **all** of the following questions.

```
┌─────────────────────────────────────────┐
│     Your answers should not be based      │
│     on work from the stimulus material.   │
└─────────────────────────────────────────┘
```

4.   Read the following and then answer the questions.

David is fun-loving and outrageous! He is sixteen and a "party animal". He has lots of friends.

Vicky wants to go into politics. She is seventeen and enjoys reading. She has a few friends — most are older than her.

Imagine that you are to design David and Vicky's "look". Describe their costume and general appearance.

(*a*) David _____

_____

_____

_____

_____

_____

6

(*b*) Vicky _____

_____

_____

_____

_____

_____

6

Marks

5. Think back to a character that you successfully portrayed in your Standard Grade Drama course.

(*a*) Describe that character.

_____

_____

_____

_____

_____

3

(*b*) List **five** characterisation techniques you used, or could have used, to develop this character.

1 _____

2 _____

3 _____

4 _____

5 _____

5

(*c*) Choose **one** from the list above and say how this technique helped you, or might have helped you, to develop a greater understanding of this character.

_____

_____

_____

_____

_____

_____

_____

4

[Turn over

	Marks

6. Write the correct word after each definition.

(a) Person who has written the play _____ **1**

(b) Sides of a theatre stage _____ **1**

(c) Actions or remarks whose significance is not realised by all the characters

_____ **1**

(d) Rising and falling of voice in speech _____ **1**

(e) Piece of scenery on wheels for ease of movement _____ **1**

(f) Slope of stage (to allow actors to be seen) _____ **1**

(g) Thin metal plate cut out in a pattern and placed in a lantern to project pattern or shape into the acting area

_____ **1**

(h) Stage fireworks _____ **1**

Marks

7. The following excerpt is from the opening scene of *Iron* by *Rona Munro*. Read it carefully and then answer the questions.

Act One

The sounds of a woman's prison just before lockdown.

GUARD 1 (*roars from offstage*). Lock down! Lock down!

Waiting room. A small area outside the visitor's room. This is where visitors wait for their names to be called. Josie is sitting here, alone. She seems unperturbed, pleasantly interested in her surroundings. Her clothes are fashionable but very low key. She wears black. She looks very plain and very expensive. She's just waiting, perfectly composed.

After a moment GUARD 2 *enters, she looks at* JOSIE *for a moment without saying anything.* JOSIE *looks back, she smiles pleasantly.*

GUARD 2. You're here to see Prisoner Black?

JOSIE. That's right.

GUARD 2 (*shaking head*). Never thought I'd see the day . . .

JOSIE. Is there a problem? You didn't call my name.

GUARD 2. So who are you?

JOSIE. Josie . . . Josie Kerr? I'm . . . She was my mother.

Pause. GUARD 2 *is completely flabbergasted.*

GUARD 2. You're her daughter?

[Turn over

7. **(continued)**

(*a*) Now focus on the **waiting room** mentioned in the script extract.

Describe the appearance of the set. You should demonstrate how the set itself, the set dressings, colours and set props reflect the room's mood and atmosphere.

The mood and atmosphere I would create in this room is _____

_____

This is how I would create it _____

_____

_____

_____

_____

_____

_____

_____

_____

_____

_____

_____

_____

_____

_____

8

Marks

7. (continued)

Look again at the dialogue between the two characters printed below and imagine that you are going to direct this scene.

GUARD 2. You're here to see Prisoner Black?

JOSIE. That's right.

GUARD 2 (*shaking head*). Never thought I'd see the day . . .

JOSIE. Is there a problem? You didn't call my name.

GUARD 2. So who are you?

JOSIE. Josie . . . Josie Kerr? I'm . . . She was my mother.

Pause. GUARD 2 is completely flabbergasted.

GUARD 2. You're her daughter?

(*b*) Make notes for the actors to assist them in their portrayal of these characters.

GUARD 2 _____

_____

_____

_____

_____

_____

_____

_____

5

JOSIE _____

_____

_____

_____

_____

_____

_____

_____

5

[END OF QUESTION PAPER]

[BLANK PAGE]

[BLANK PAGE]

[BLANK PAGE]

[BLANK PAGE]

Acknowledgements

Leckie and Leckie is grateful to the copyright holders, as credited, for permission to use their material.
The Oscar Marzaroli Collection for a photograph (2004 Stimulus paper p 3); 'The Scream' by Edvard Munch © The Munch Museum / The Munch-Ellingsen Group / DACS 2008

 'Flight' by Quint Buchholz © DACS 2007. Leckie and Leckie has paid DACS' visual creators for the use of their artistic works.(2007 Stimulus paper p 2);

Nick Hern Books for an extract from 'Iron' by Rona Munro (2008 Credit paper p 7)

The following companies have very generously given permission to reproduce their copyright material free of charge:
Steve Savage Publishers for the proverb 'Wha daur bell the cat?' (2004 Stimulus paper p 2);
International Creative Management, Inc for an extract from The Crucible by Arthur Miller (2005 Stimulus paper p 4).
Nick Hern Books for an extract from 'Wormwood' by Catherine Czerkawska, taken from Scottish Plays (2006 Stimulus paper p 4).
Alan Brodie Representation Ltd for an extract from 'Men should weep' by Ena Lamont Stewart (2008 Stimulus paper p 4)